Blastoff! Readers are carefully developed by literacy experts to build reading stamina and move students toward fluency by combining standards-based content with developmentally appropriate text.

Level 1 provides the most support through repetition of high-frequency words, light text, predictable sentence patterns, and strong visual support.

Level 2 offers early readers a bit more challenge through varied sentences, increased text load, and text-supportive special features.

Level 3 advances early-fluent readers toward fluency through increased text load, less reliance on photos, advancing concepts, longer sentences, and more complex special features.

★ **Blastoff! Universe**

Reading Level: Blastoff! Beginners (Grade K) → Blastoff! Readers (Grades 1–3) → Blastoff! Discovery (Grade 4)

This edition first published in 2024 by Bellwether Media, Inc.

No part of this publication may be reproduced in whole or in part without written permission of the publisher. For information regarding permission, write to Bellwether Media, Inc., Attention: Permissions Department, 6012 Blue Circle Drive, Minnetonka, MN 55343.

Library of Congress Cataloging-in-Publication Data

Names: Anderson, Shannon, 1972- author.
Title: Argentina / by Shannon Anderson.
Description: Minneapolis, MN : Bellwether Media, Inc., 2024. | Series: Blastoff! Readers : countries of the world | Includes bibliographical references and index. | Audience: Ages 5-8 | Audience: Grades 2-3 | Summary: "Relevant images match informative text in this introduction to Argentina. Intended for students in kindergarten through third grade"– Provided by publisher.
Identifiers: LCCN 2023003644 (print) | LCCN 2023003645 (ebook) | ISBN 9798886874280 (library binding) | ISBN 9798886876161 (ebook)
Subjects: LCSH: Argentina–Juvenile literature.
Classification: LCC F2808.2 .A53 2024 (print) | LCC F2808.2 (ebook) | DDC 982–dc23/eng/20230126
LC record available at https://lccn.loc.gov/2023003644
LC ebook record available at https://lccn.loc.gov/2023003645

Text copyright © 2024 by Bellwether Media, Inc. BLASTOFF! READERS and associated logos are trademarks and/or registered trademarks of Bellwether Media, Inc.

Editor: Rebecca Sabelko   Designer: Gabriel Hilger

Printed in the United States of America, North Mankato, MN.

Table of Contents

All About Argentina	4
Land and Animals	6
Life in Argentina	12
Argentina Facts	20
Glossary	22
To Learn More	23
Index	24

All About Argentina

Buenos Aires

Argentina is a long country in South America. Its capital is Buenos Aires.

The country is home to one of the southernmost cities in the world!

Buenos Aires, Argentina

Land and Animals

Scrubland covers northern Argentina. The central Pampas are **grasslands**.

A **plateau** makes up Patagonia in the south. Huge **glaciers** cover some of this land. Mountains line the west.

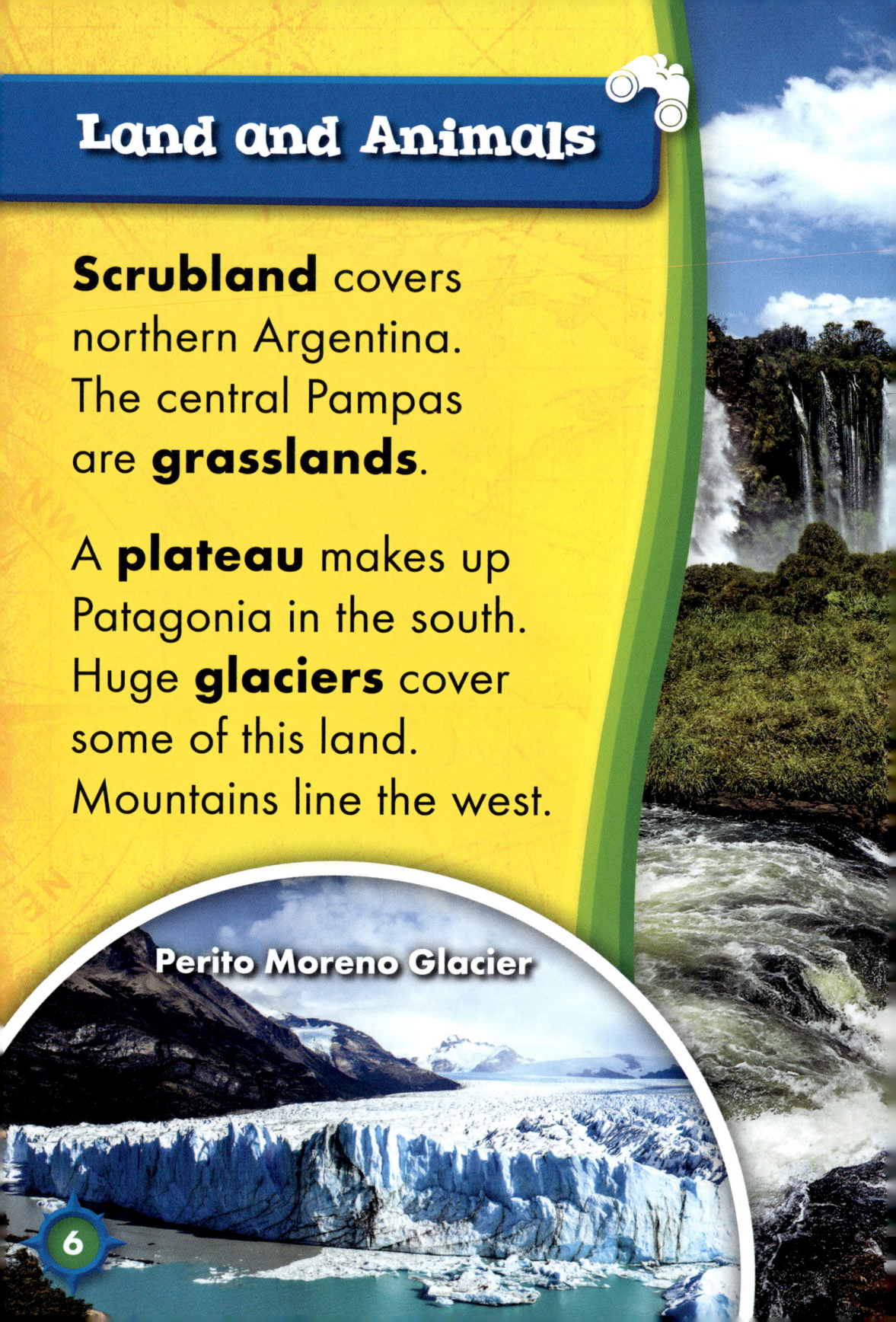

Perito Moreno Glacier

Iguazú Falls

Size: up to 269 feet (82 meters) tall
Famous For: made up of 275 waterfalls that make a horseshoe shape

Pampas

The country's **climate** is mostly **temperate**. Northeastern Argentina gets the most rain.

Patagonia and the mountains can get very cold.

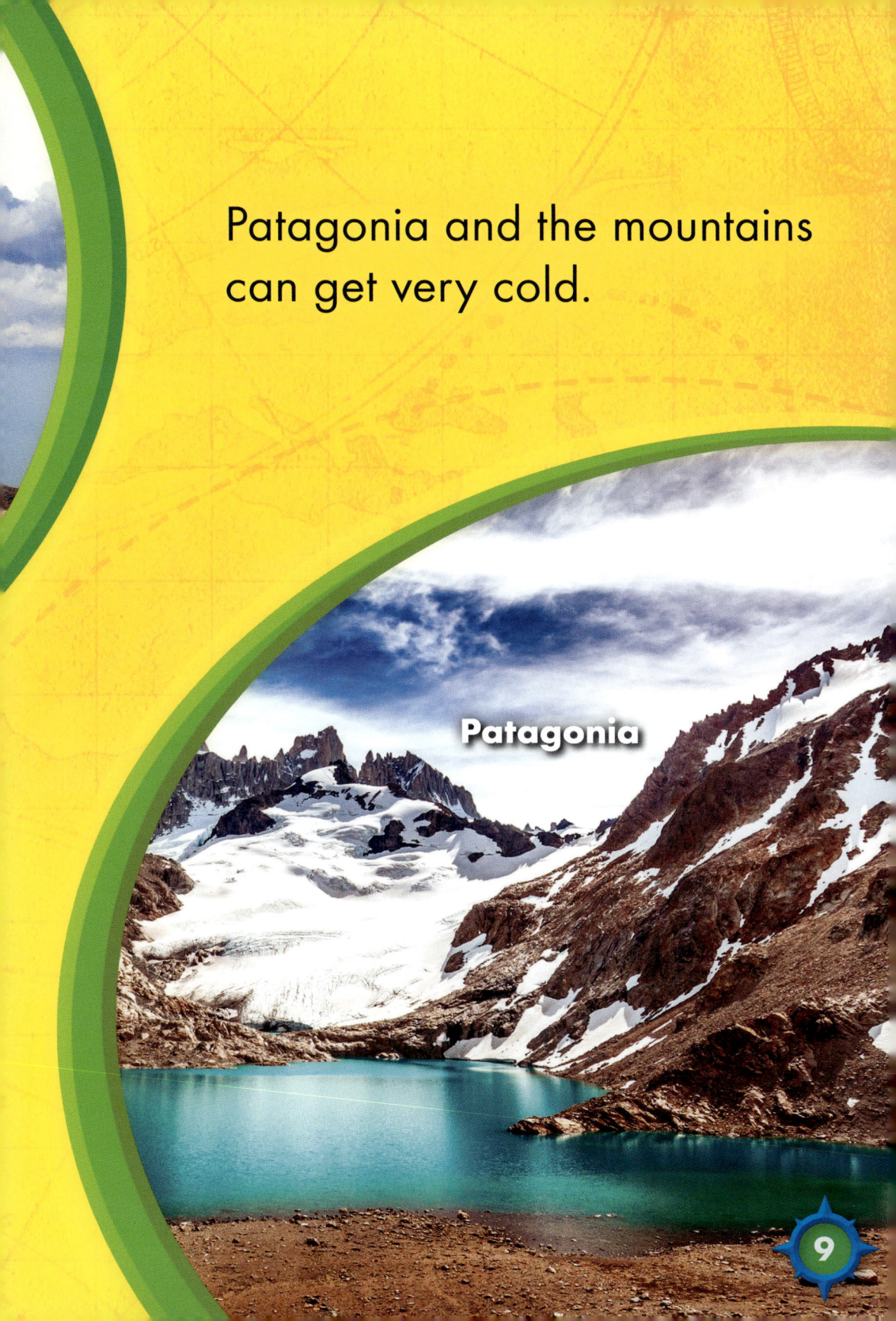

Patagonia

Guanacos eat grass in the mountains. Capybaras live where it is wet.

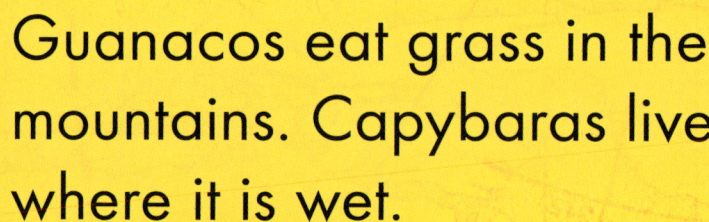
guanacos

Penguins raise young on the southern shores. Seals hunt fish off the coast.

Life in Argentina

People who live in Argentina are called Argentines. Most people speak Spanish.

Over half of all Argentines are **Catholics**. Most people live in the cities.

Buenos Aires

tango

The tango is popular. It is a type of music and dance from Argentina.

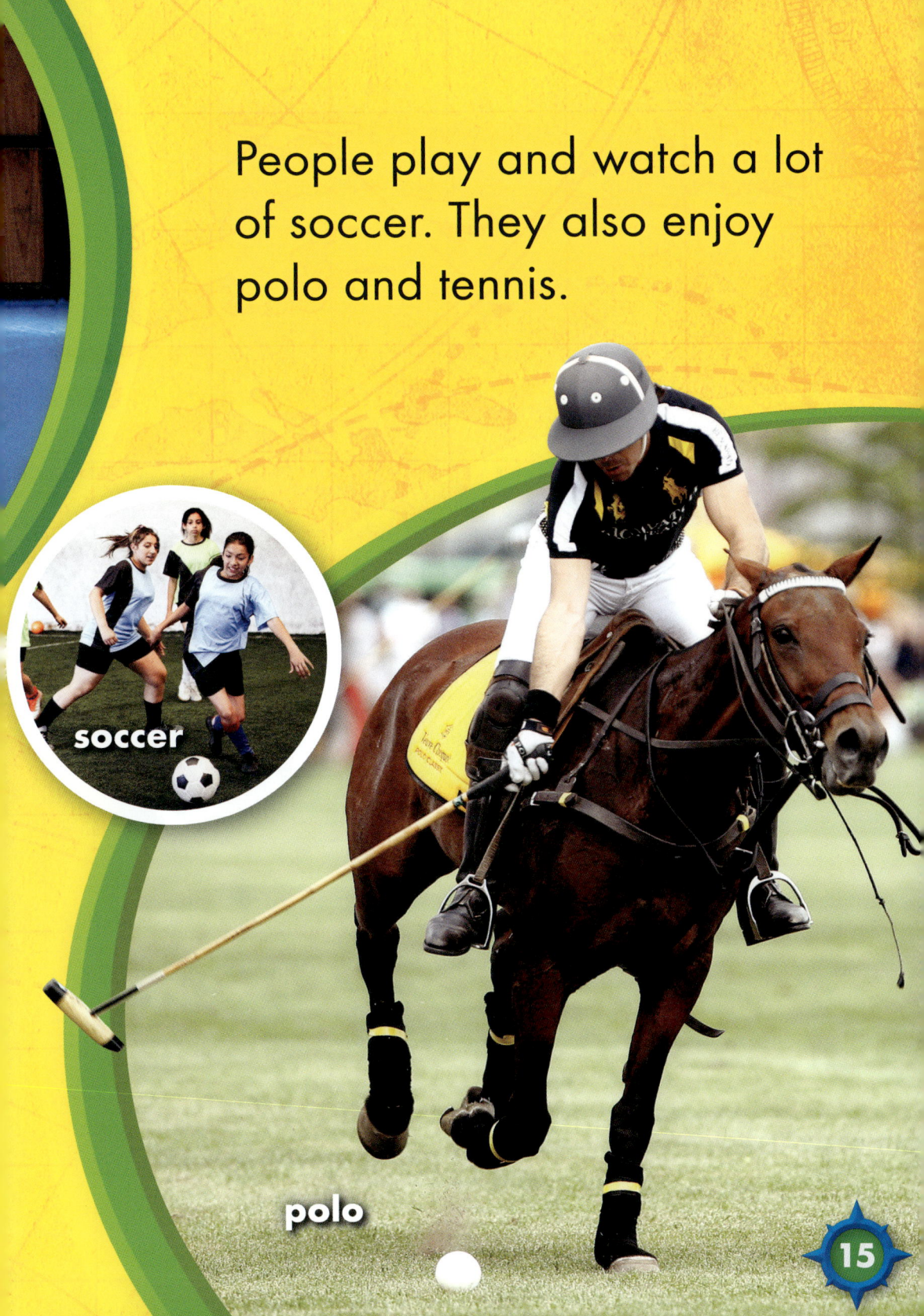

People play and watch a lot of soccer. They also enjoy polo and tennis.

soccer

polo

Sweet rolls are a favorite breakfast food. Empanadas are filled pastries. They make easy snacks.

Argentine Foods

sweet rolls

empanadas

grilled beef

mate

Grilled beef is common during meals. People drink a tea called *mate* from a **gourd**.

El Carnaval

Argentina's national holiday is Revolution Day on May 25.

People enjoy *El Carnaval* in summer. They dance at parades. Argentines have a lot to **celebrate**!

Argentina Facts

Size:
1,073,518 square miles
(2,780,400 square kilometers)

Population:
46,245,668

National Holiday:
Revolution Day (May 25)

Main Language:
Spanish

Capital City:
Buenos Aires

Famous Face

Name: Lionel Messi

Famous For: soccer player who has won the World Cup and seven Ballon d'Ors

Religions

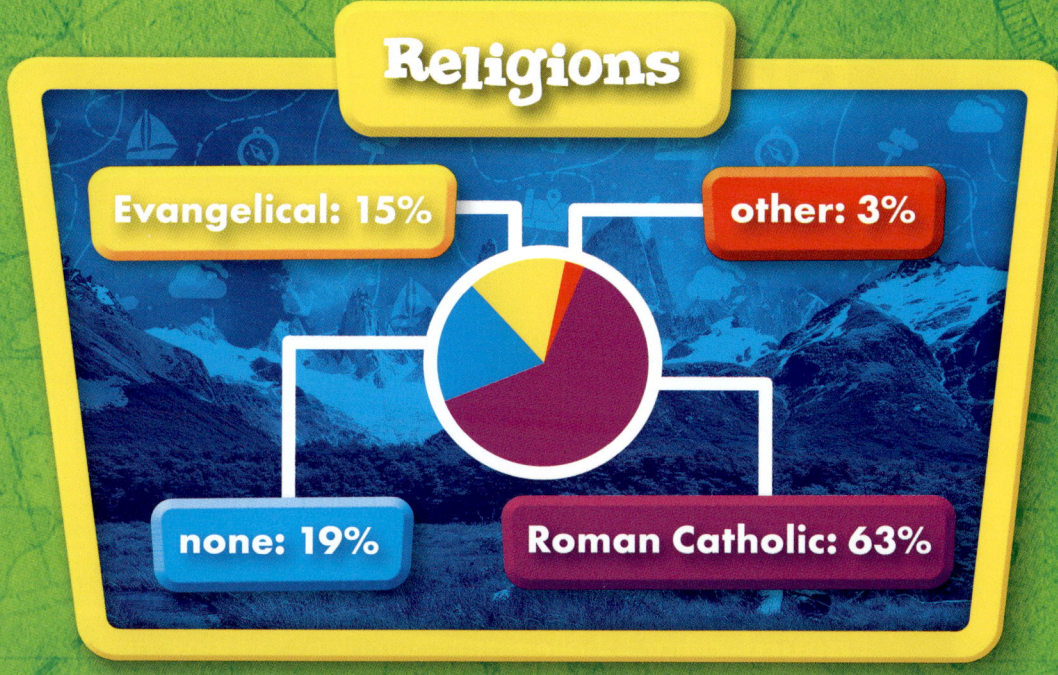

- Evangelical: 15%
- other: 3%
- none: 19%
- Roman Catholic: 63%

Top Landmarks

Mount Aconcagua

Perito Moreno Glacier

Valdes Peninsula

Glossary

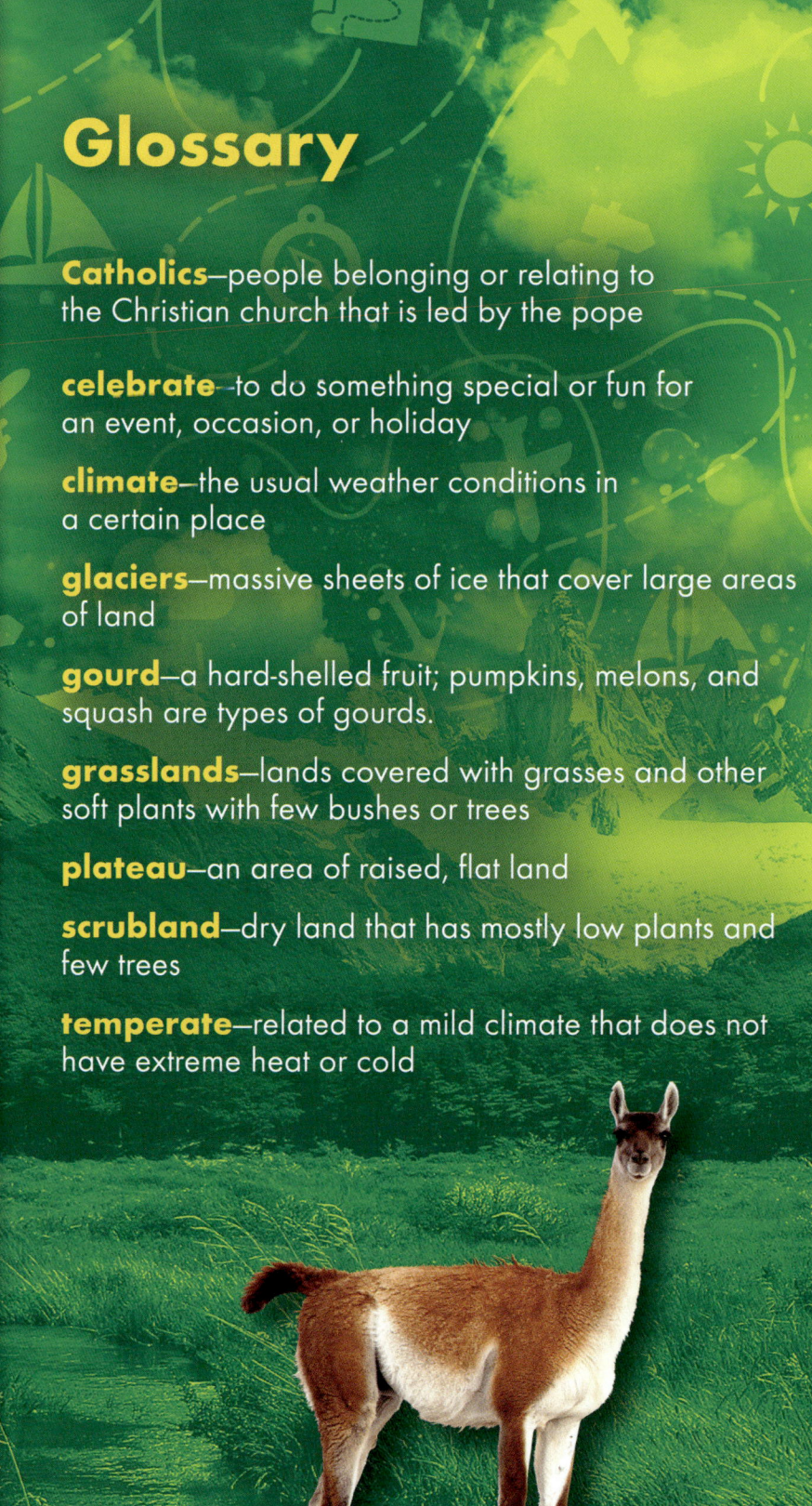

Catholics—people belonging or relating to the Christian church that is led by the pope

celebrate—to do something special or fun for an event, occasion, or holiday

climate—the usual weather conditions in a certain place

glaciers—massive sheets of ice that cover large areas of land

gourd—a hard-shelled fruit; pumpkins, melons, and squash are types of gourds.

grasslands—lands covered with grasses and other soft plants with few bushes or trees

plateau—an area of raised, flat land

scrubland—dry land that has mostly low plants and few trees

temperate—related to a mild climate that does not have extreme heat or cold

To Learn More

AT THE LIBRARY

Grack, Rachel. *Capybaras*. Minneapolis, Minn.: Bellwether Media, 2019.

Markovics, Joyce. *Argentina*. New York, N.Y.: Bearport Publishing, 2019.

Spanier, Kristine. *Argentina*. Minneapolis, Minn.: Jump!, 2020.

ON THE WEB

FACTSURFER

Factsurfer.com gives you a safe, fun way to find more information.

1. Go to www.factsurfer.com.

2. Enter "Argentina" into the search box and click 🔍.

3. Select your book cover to see a list of related content.

Index

animals, 10, 11
Argentina facts, 20–21
Buenos Aires, 4, 5, 12
capital (see Buenos Aires)
Catholics, 12
cities, 5, 12
climate, 8
coast, 11
dance, 14, 19
El Carnaval, 18, 19
food, 16, 17
glaciers, 6
grasslands, 6
Iguazú Falls, 7
map, 5
mountains, 6, 9, 10
music, 14
Pampas, 6, 8
Patagonia, 6, 9

people, 12, 15, 17, 19
plateau, 6
polo, 15
rain, 8
Revolution Day, 18
say hello, 13
scrubland, 6
soccer, 15
South America, 4
Spanish, 12, 13
tango, 14
tennis, 15

The images in this book are reproduced through the courtesy of: saiko3p, front cover; Det-anan, front cover; Carolina Jaramillo, p. 3; DiegoCityExplorer, pp. 4-5; Ezg, p. 6; Just Your Suitcase, pp. 6-7; Pablo Rodriguez Merkel, pp. 8-9; javarman, p. 9; Jota.designstudio, pp. 10-11; Mariana Zalvidea, p. 11 (guanaco); sunsinger, p. 11 (capybara); Ondrej Prosicy, p. 11 (Magellanic penguin); Gabriel Rojo, p. 11 (southern elephant seal); diegograndi, p. 12; Tempura, pp. 12-13; holgs, pp. 14-15; Porta/ Getty Images, p. 15 (soccer); Debby Wong, p. 15 (polo); Florentine, p. 16 (sweet rolls); Alexandr Vorobev, p. 16 (empanadas); Foodio, p. 16 (grilled beef); Africa Studio, p. 16 (*mate*); cristiani, p. 17; Collab Media, pp. 18-19; titoOnz, p. 20 (flag); Asatur Yesayants, p. 20 (Lionel Messi); GC photographer, p. 21 (Mount Aconcagua); TheEverywhereMan, p. 21 (Perito Moreno Glacier); Ticiana Giehl, p. 21 (Valdes Peninsula); buteo, p. 22.